NASCAR!
★ AN IMAGINATION LIBRARY SERIES ★

Southern 500

by Eric Ethan

Gareth Stevens Publishing
MILWAUKEE

The author wishes to thank Glen Fitzgerald, George Philips, Mary Jo Lindahl, and Juanita Jones for their help and encouragement.

For a free color catalog describing Gareth Stevens Publishing's list of high-quality books and multimedia programs, call 1-800-542-2595 (USA) or 1-800-461-9120 (Canada). Gareth Stevens Publishing's Fax: (414) 225-0377.

Library of Congress Cataloging-in-Publication Data

Ethan, Eric.
    Southern 500 / by Eric Ethan.
      p. cm. — (NASCAR! an imagination library series)
    Includes index.
    Summary: Describes the Southern 500, one of the oldest races sponsored by the National Association for Stock Car Auto Racing (NASCAR) and held annually in Darlington, South Carolina.
    ISBN 0-8368-2140-8 (lib. bdg.)
    1. Southern 500 (Automobile race)—Juvenile literature. 2. Stock car racing—United States—Juvenile literature. [1. Southern 500 (Automobile race). 2. Stock car racing.] I. Title. II. Series: Ethan, Eric. NASCAR! an imagination library series.
    GV1033.5.S68E85   1999
    796.72'06'875766—dc21   99-14634

First published in North America in 1999 by
Gareth Stevens Publishing
1555 North RiverCenter Drive, Suite 201
Milwaukee, WI 53212 USA

This edition © 1999 by Gareth Stevens, Inc. Text by Eric Ethan. Photographs © 1998: Cover, pp. 11, 13, 19 - Don Grassman; pp. 15, 17 - Sammy Kosh; pp. 5, 7, 21 - Ernest Masche. Illustration: p. 9 - The Official NASCAR Preview and Press Guide. Additional end matter © 1999 by Gareth Stevens, Inc.

Text: Eric Ethan
Page layout: Lesley M. White
Cover design: Lesley M. White
Editorial assistant: Diane Laska

Printed in the United States of America

1 2 3 4 5 6 7 8 9 03 02 01 00 99

TABLE OF CONTENTS

Metric Chart
1 mile = 1.609 kilometers
100 miles = 160.9 km
500 miles = 804.5 km

Words that appear in the glossary are printed in
boldface type the first time they occur in the text.

THE SOUTHERN 500

The Southern 500 is one of NASCAR's oldest races. NASCAR stands for the National Association for Stock Car Auto Racing. The Southern 500 was first run in 1950. Johnny Mantz won the first race, driving a 1950 Plymouth at an average speed of 76 miles per hour. It took drivers almost seven hours to complete the race that year. That is very slow when compared to today's race speeds.

In 1993, Mark Martin won the Southern 500 with an average speed of 137.93 miles per hour. Driving nearly twice as fast as Mantz in 1950, Martin finished the race in just over 3½ hours. Jeff Gordon won in 1995, 1996, 1997, and 1998. This is a great accomplishment in the highly competitive world of motor sports.

These spectators enjoy a view of the straightaway and pit row at the 1998 Southern 500.
CIA Stock Photo: Ernest Masche

DARLINGTON RACEWAY

The Southern 500 takes place the first weekend in September every year at the Darlington Raceway near Darlington, South Carolina. The raceway was built in 1949 and is one of the oldest tracks on the NASCAR circuit. It has been modified for faster cars and to allow more fans to attend. In 1997, a new state-of-the-art tower grandstand was built. The track can now seat over seventy thousand fans.

Darlington Raceway also houses the NMPA Stock Car Hall of Fame/Joe Weatherly Museum. NMPA stands for the National Motorsports Press Association. Joe Weatherly, a NASCAR driver, died in a crash during a race in 1964. The museum contains a priceless collection of historic NASCAR race cars and NASCAR driver memorabilia.

Dale Jarrett leads the pack at the 1998 Southern 500 just after the start of the race.
CIA Stock Photo: Ernest Masche

THE TRACK

The Darlington Raceway is oval shaped with one end of the oval wider than the other. This track has been called "too tough to tame" by many drivers. The course is a short 1.366 miles, but cars can still reach very high speeds. A single-lap speed record of 173.797 miles per hour was set by Ward Burton in 1996.

All of the turns at Darlington Raceway are **banked**, with the outside of the track higher than the inner edge. This keeps cars from flying off the track, allowing them to travel around the track at high speed.

The Darlington Raceway has a unique oval shape.

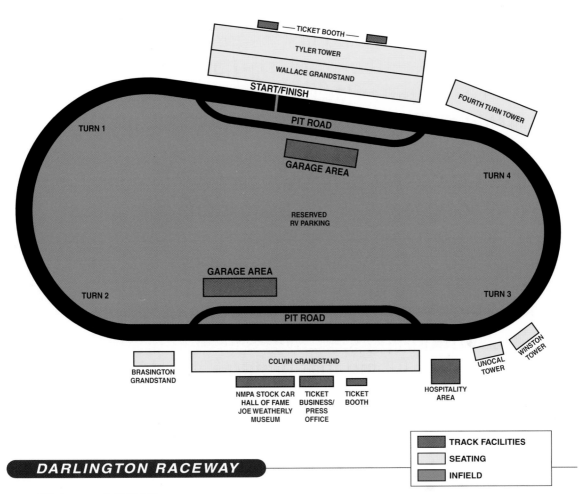

DARLINGTON RACEWAY

Distance: 1.366 Miles

Banking: Turns 1 & 2 — 25 degrees, Turns 3 & 4 — 23 degrees

Qualifying Record: Ward Burton, 173.797 mph (28.295 seconds), set March 22, 1996

Race Record (500 Miles): Dale Earnhardt, 139.958 mph, set March 28, 1993

NASCAR RACERS

When NASCAR racing first began in 1948, racers drove late-model **stock cars** sold by regular automobile dealers. Racing teams removed the hubcaps, added a seat belt and a number, and the cars were ready to go.

Today's NASCAR cars are built from the ground up by each racing team. Each team starts with a cast-iron motor from one of the major automobile makers, such as Ford or Chevrolet. The rest of the frame is built by hand from metal tubing. Although the tubing is lightweight, the complete welded frame is very strong. Surrounding the driver's seat is a special **roll cage** of heavier tubing that protects the driver in case of an accident.

Driver Dale Jarrett waits for mechanics to finish working on his car before the start of the 1998 Southern 500.
CIA Stock Photo: Don Grassman

DRIVERS AND TEAMS

Ernie Irvan drives car number 36, sponsored by Skittles candy. He has been driving since 1987 and has won over fifteen NASCAR races. His winnings totaled almost $11 million through the 1998 season.

Drivers actually work for racing teams and their owners. Team owners hire the best drivers they can find. The owners also bring together mechanics and the **pit crew**. Drivers and all of the team members need to work together smoothly to win races.

NASCAR racing is very expensive. Sponsors pay money to team owners to have their **logos** displayed on the cars.

Ernie Irvan passes Jeff Burton on the outside, late in the running of the 1998 Southern 500.
CIA Stock Photo: Don Grassman

Besides winning money for their teams, drivers also win points each time they race. NASCAR's driver point system gives winners 175 points. Second place and the rest of the finishers get fewer and fewer points, with the last-place driver getting 43 points.

At the end of each racing season, NASCAR drivers are ranked by the total number of points they have. The driver with the most points becomes the Winston Cup Driver of the Year, which brings a lot of prestige to his team. Top-ranked teams have an easier time finding sponsors to finance them.

Jeff Gordon, winner of multiple Southern 500 races, was also the Winston Cup Driver of the Year in 1995, 1997, and 1998.

Winner Jeff Gordon takes his victory lap at the 1998 Southern 500.
CIA Stock Photo: Sammy Kosh

QUALIFYING

Qualifying takes place two days before race day. This event gives drivers and mechanics a chance to learn the track and determine what adjustments need to be made to their cars. NASCAR race cars have many different parts that can be changed to suit a racetrack. Tire pressure, steering, and the suspension can be adjusted to make the cars perform even better.

Once drivers and teams have made practice laps and adjustments, the drivers are ready to qualify. Each driver travels once around the track at the fastest speed possible. The fastest car secures the best starting position for the actual race. That car is awarded the **pole** – the inside, front position.

The outer edge of the Darlington Raceway is banked to help the cars corner.
CIA Stock Photo: Sammy Kosh

RACE DAY

On race day, the cars line up in qualifying order. Then, they circle the track again and again. They build up speed, lap after lap. When the race **starter** drops the green flag, the cars in the front row pull away from the pack. This is called a flying start.

Drivers quickly try to settle into a **groove**, or the position on the track that best allows drivers to enter and leave the corners the quickest. Drivers often follow other cars very closely. This is called **drafting**. The car behind uses less fuel to travel just as fast as the car in front, but its motor doesn't have to work as hard. Champion drivers race lap after lap for hours in tightly packed groups of cars.

An accident occurred early in the race at the 1998 Southern 500.
CIA Stock Photo: Don Grassman

ACTION IN THE PITS

Part of racing strategy is knowing when to stop for fuel and new tires. When cars go into the pit, other cars can get ahead of them. So, drivers pay close attention to when other cars leave the track. If the race leader stops, other drivers may decide to do the same. The other drivers know the leader probably can't get farther ahead of them if they make pit stops at the same time.

Getting in and out of the pits quickly can mean the difference between winning and losing. A race team practices for hours and hours to be able to refuel the car, change tires, and clean the windshield in under a minute. Team crew chiefs organize the pit crew so that each person in the pit has a single job and becomes an expert at doing it.

Driver Dale Earnhardt, Jr.'s pit crew works feverishly to get him back on the track during the 1998 Southern 500.
CIA Stock Photo: Ernest Masche

SAFETY

NASCAR racing can be a dangerous sport. Drivers and spectators know accidents happen, but many precautions are taken to prevent them. All professional NASCAR drivers, even the new drivers called rookies, have many years of racing experience. NASCAR race cars have fire-extinguishing equipment and roll cages to protect the driver in case of an accident.

Safety is also important for race fans. Modern race courses have special retaining walls and fences to stop cars and debris from flying into the crowd. Elevated grandstands keep people above the action and hopefully out of the path of the cars and debris.

GLOSSARY

You can find these words on the pages listed. Reading a word in a sentence helps you understand it even better.

banked — inclined upward from the inside edge 8

drafting (DRAF-ting) — when one car follows closely behind another during a race to save fuel and engine wear 18

groove — the part of a racetrack that is best for going into corners and coming out onto the straightaways 18

logos (LOW-gos) — graphic designs that feature the name or product of a company 12

pit crew — a team of workers that maintains a race car off the track during a race 12, 20

pole — the inside, front spot in a car race 16

qualifying (KWAH-lih-fy-ing) — a test that makes a person or object fit for a certain position 16, 18

roll cage — a framework of metal bars that encloses and protects the driver 10, 22

starter — a person who signals the beginning of a race 18

stock cars — new-model sedans manufactured by Detroit automakers, such as Ford, General Motors, and Chevrolet 4, 6, 10

PLACES TO WRITE

International Motor Sports Museum
Public Relations Manager
3198 Speedway Boulevard
Talladega, AL 35160

Daytona USA
Public Relations Manager
1801 West International Boulevard
Daytona Beach, FL 32114

Motorbooks International
Public Relations Manager
729 Prospect Avenue/Box 1
Osceola, WI 54020

Russell Branham, Public Relations Director
Darlington Raceway
1301 Harry Byrd Highway/Box 500
Darlington, SC 29532

WEB SITES

www.nascar.com

This is the official web site of the National Association for Stock Car Auto Racing.

www.ciastockphoto.com

This is one of the best NASCAR photo sites. It is the source of many of the pictures in this book. It presents new images during each racing season.

racing.yahoo.com/rac/nascar

At this web site, race fans can find current NASCAR race results, standings, schedules, driver profiles, feature stories, and merchandise.

Due to the dynamic nature of the Internet, some web sites stay current longer than others. To find additional web sites, use a reliable search engine with one or more of the following keywords: *Darlington Raceway, Jeff Gordon, Joe Weatherly Museum, Mark Martin, NASCAR, NMPA Stock Car Hall of Fame,* and *Southern 500.*

INDEX

DATE DUE

DEMCO